Com

Custo

MW01292641

Improve Your Job Skills

&

Provide A Great Customer Experience

by

Victoria Wells

Published by Geezer Guides

Copyright 2013 Victoria Wells

ISBN-13: 978-1482746150

ISBN-10: 1482746158

CONTENTS

CHAPTER 1
BASIC CUSTOMER SERVICE CONCEPTS

In Chapter 1 we'll learn some basic customer service concepts. And, like the title of this book suggests, it's pretty much common sense.

➤ *How the "Do Unto Others" principle applies to customer service.*

➤ *Is the customer always right?*

DO UNTO OTHERS

We've all heard about the Golden Rule and, it seems, it is a concept that has been embraced by many cultures throughout history. Wikipedia has a good account of this pervasive ideology. Just go to Wikipedia.com and search for Golden Rule. Apparently there are references to this philosophy all the way back to ancient Babylon.

http://en.wikipedia.org/wiki/Golden_rule

The underlying principle of basic, common sense customer service is expressed well by the Golden Rule - do unto others as you would have them do unto you.

I know that seems rather simplified, but think about it for a minute. When you're expecting exceptional customer service for a product or service that you've purchased, or are considering purchasing, don't you expect the customer service person to deal with you fairly and with respect? Isn't that how you feel you should treat your customers?

If you don't feel that the majority of your customers deserve fairness and respect, you may be in the wrong field.

You'll find that this conviction is a recurring theme throughout this book.

THE CUSTOMER IS ALWAYS RIGHT - NOT!

Who coined the phrase "The customer is always right."? Take a look at the website phrases.org.uk and search on the phrase "The customer is always right." You'll find some interesting history on this oft-used term.

http://www.phrases.org.uk/meanings/106700.html

"The customer is always right" is a phrase that we have all heard over and over again . Well, it's time to clear up this oft-quoted misconception.

Many customers, as you probably already know, can be unreasonable and demanding. They expect to get whatever they want because they believe they are entitled, simply because they are the customer.

I'm sorry, but the customer is NOT always right. I'll give you a big hint, too. They often KNOW they aren't right, but will try it on for size anyway.

THE CUSTOMER IS ALWAYS THE CUSTOMER

However, having said that, what I do believe, is that the customer is always the customer and should be treated with respect. After all, if you don't have any customers, you don't have a business. So, whether you're an owner, a manager or an employee, without customers there is no income and with no income there are no jobs. That's something to seriously think about.

Now, there are times, and these times are rare, that certain customers don't even deserve your respect. You know the ones I mean. They are downright abusive. We'll explore how to deal with such customers later in this book. (See Chapter 5 - Dealing with Different Types of Customers)

However, for now, remember that your customer is your income. You want them to be happy, but it needs to be a win-win situation - something that both you and your customer can accept and live with.

We'll learn more about win-win situations later in this book.

In Chapter 1 we have learned a couple of key customer service concepts:

✔ *If you treat a customer the way you, yourself would like to be treated then you are most certainly on the right track to excellent customer service.*

✔ *Although a customer is NOT always right, they are always your customer and they deserve to be treated with respect (with only a few exceptions).*

CHAPTER 2
ATTITUDE AND PERSONALITY

In Chapter 2 we'll learn about the type of personalities that seem to the customer service field. You may have noticed that, in ge come across the same personality types. This isn't a coincidence. A customer service seems to attract, and keep, people with similar:

 *Personalities*

 *Attitudes*

PERSONALITY

According to Wikipedia - http://en.wikipedia.org/wiki/Personality:

> *Personality is the particular combination of emotional, attitudinal, and behavioral response patterns of an individual.*

You've probably heard that it takes a certain type of person to work in customer service. And you know what? It's true.

Certain personalities simply do better in this kind of position than others. And, although it may sound sexist, frequently it's women that excel in a customer service environment.

No, I'm not saying that men don't do well in customer service. Of course they do. But you are more likely to find that women are drawn to this profession.

Truly, I am not trying to be sexist here. However, I am writing this book from my own point of view and experiences. And, I'm a woman who has spent over 30 years in customer service - as a customer service rep, as an employer of customer service personnel and as a customer service consultant.

You may find that in the more technical fields, you'll see more men, but that has been changing rapidly and you are now likely to find a more equitable mix in those fields as well.

In most cases, the type of attitude you'll find in good customer service people is a can-do, let's make everyone happy kind of outlook.

A good customer service person isn't looking to triumph over a customer, they genuinely hope to create a win-win situation. They are actively looking to find solutions that are good for both their company and their customer. That way everyone is happy.

...d it doesn't always happen. But that's what a
... be striving to achieve.

...diator at times. The company, who pays your
...cern to your future employment. The customer,
...ducts, is of great concern as well. If they stop
...icts, then the company may go out of business

...e, and you need to do it with a calm and positive

It you ... , to win, and someone else needs to lose, then you might want to look at other types of jobs because the odds are you won't excel at customer service.

"*Personal Anecdote*"

My experience as both an employee and a consultant has been mostly in the technical field with such diverse companies as a packaging machinery company, a flexible metal hose company, a company that supplies soot-blowers to pulp and paper mills, a company that manufactures automated gluing machines, a company that manufacturers powder paint coating equipment and a software development company.

One company, where I applied for a technical customer service position early in my career, was very candid with me about the selection process after I was hired. They were certain they were looking for a man for the position, someone with a technical and mechanical background.

They told me that they created three piles from all the resumés they had received. The A pile contained, in their estimation, the most qualified candidates. The B pile contained the next most qualified. And, the C pile contained those who they felt were not suited for the position and would, most likely, not be called for an interview.

A few months after I was hired, I was told that, even though they thought I had the qualifications of the A pile, my resumé had been placed in the B pile. Why? Because they were sure they needed a man for the position and I was a woman.

Fortunately I thrived in the position and, it seems, that I was able to change their attitude towards hiring women. While I was still there, as manager of the department, we hired several more people, including women. This was a totally new concept for this company but by changing their attitude they hired many more qualified people, both men and women.

By the time I left the ratio was still about 3 to 1 – 3 men for every 1 woman - but that was a big change from the idea that the department should be 100% men.

I guess what I'm try to convey here is - look at the qualifications, not the gender.

ATTITUDE

According to Wikipedia - http://en.wikipedia.org/wiki/Attitude:

> *Attitude is a person's perspective toward a specified target and way of saying and doing things.*

Just as personality can make a difference between a mediocre customer service person and a great one, attitude plays a large role as well.

It helps if you've got that "bubbly" attitude towards life if you're considering a career in customer service.

We've all experienced the difference between a genuinely happy person and one that's forcing themselves to even talk to you. How many times have you walked away from an encounter with a dour customer service person thinking "boy, are they in the wrong job"?

Attitude is something that comes with being happy, or unhappy, with yourself, your job, your life. And many times you need to adopt both a professional and a private attitude. What I mean by that is that you need to leave work at work and home at home. Your customers should not hear about any problems you might have at home. And I'm not even talking about specifically complaining to a customer about problems in your personal life. What I'm talking about is attitude "leakage", if you will. Letting personal problems color your work attitude. Your customers should never know if you've had a spat with your significant other, not by what you say or by the attitude you project. Don't be surly with a customer because you're upset with someone or something in your personal life. If you want a career in customer service, you need to be professional - all day, every day.

On the flip side, that goes for your personal life, too. Sure customers will upset you, frustrate you and even make you question your career choice. But don't take that with you when you leave work and enter back into your personal life. Leave work at work.

No, this is not easy. It is a learned skill, not one that comes naturally. You need to work at it - both professionally and personally. But the more you work at it, the easier it is to separate your work life from your private life. And, believe me, BOTH will benefit.

In Chapter 2 we have learned the importance of both personality and attitude in a customer service profession.

✔ *Did you see yourself here?*

✔ *Did you commit to the concept of leaving home at home and work at work?*

✔ *Do you think you've got what it takes - personality and attitude - to be an exceptional customer service person?*

Chapter 3
General telephone basics

In Chapter 3 we'll learn how to stay in touch with our customers by phone.

This chapter is dedicated exclusively to customer contact by telephone because telephone skills are exceptionally important.

Nowadays, most contact, except perhaps in retail, is made either by telephone or email. However, even brick and mortar stores are now making great strides in using both the telephone and email to stay in touch with their customers.

In this chapter we'll learn about:

➤ *Automated attendants*

➤ *Answering telephone call correctly*

➤ *The importance of returning voice messages*

Automated Attendant or Not?

I've never kept it a secret that I am no fan of automated attendants. Actually, I'm not sure of anyone who is. However, it's now become rare to call a company and encounter a "real" person answering the phone.

We've all experienced getting lost in "voicemail hell". At times the decision trees built into some of the automated attendants seem to defy logic. And, often, the choices you're expected to make are not clear. Do you press 1 for accounts or 2 for customer service or 3 for support? What if your question doesn't fit neatly into any of the available options?

What really ticks me off is when you can't get a real person at all. Often, in frustration, I will repeatedly press the "0" key in the hopes of getting a receptionist who can listen to my problem and direct me accordingly. It really upsets me when I get told that pressing "0" is not a valid option.

What this all boils down to is, don't have an automated attendant as your first line - have it as a back up if everyone else is busy.

Pick Up The Phone!

In a worst-case scenario, a customer is confronted with an automated attendant, fights their way through all the decisions trees and FINALLY gets through to (hopefully) the right person - only to get that person's voicemail!

No! No! No! If you are at your desk - **PICK UP THE PHONE!**

That is a rule I try to get implemented when I am consulting with companies and it has often been met with considerable resistance. I've heard all of the excuses, "I'm too busy to pick up the phone.", "I'm in the middle of something.", "I like to screen my calls.", and so on ...

I'm sorry, if you're in customer service you should never be too busy to talk to a customer. If you're in the middle of something else, it can wait. And screening your calls? Really? I see no need to do this in a business. It only frustrates the customer.

The only good reasons for letting a customer's call go to voicemail are:

❖ *You are away from your desk - or -*

❖ *You are already on the phone with a customer.*

PHYSICAL TELEPHONE MESSAGE RECORDS

One thing that I really like about having a "real" receptionist is having written messages. Yes, I know that's "old school" but it can also be a lifesaver. I particularly recommend the message pads that automatically make a copy of each written message. You know the one's I mean. You can tear off the message to give to the appropriate person but a copy of the message remains in the book.

Why do I like these? Well, have you ever lost a message? Have you ever accidentally deleted a voicemail message? You get the idea. It's a fallback. And, it's one I've used many times myself. You can flip back through all the message copies and find what you need.

Important: When using this type of message keeping, be sure to fill out the form fully - name of person, phone number, date and the reason the person was calling, if they share that information with the receptionist.

"PERSONAL ANECDOTE"

I'm afraid I've made myself very unpopular at some companies that I have consulted with. Usually the first thing I recommend is that they remove the automated attendant as their first line of contact. Such a recommendation can be very unpopular with some employees.

If your company doesn't actually have a dedicated receptionist then an auto-attendant may be necessary. However, there have been several companies that I have consulted with that did have receptionists on staff, however some of those receptionists didn't think that actually answering the phone should be part of their job description. I was totally taken aback. Isn't that one of the key parts of a receptionist's job?

In one particular case, though, the receptionist welcomed the change and happily answered the phone. That receptionist enjoyed the interaction with the callers and gave a very, very good first impression of the company. She was complimented many times for her attitude (always cheerful), her helpfulness and her professionalism. It was a win-win-win situation. A win for the receptionist who felt more valued in her position, a win for the company who was now projecting a much more friendly and professional profile from the time the phone was answered and a win for the customer who got a "real, live person" to help them get to whoever they needed.

SETTING UP YOUR AUTOMATED ATTENDANT

If you must use an automated attendant, then be sure you're making it easy for your customer to select the correct options. How many times have you been presented with a multitude of choices from an automated attendant but were at a loss as to which option was right for you?

The key to making the choices easy for your customers is to keep them as simple as possible. That means presenting the customer with as few choices as possible so they're not left guessing.

Many companies call their customer service departments by many different names. Things like sales, customer support, technical support, accounts receivable and so on. Make it easy for a customer to choose correctly.

If your sales department is also your customer service department - call it Sales & Customer Service. If your technical support department is also your customer service department - call it Technical Support & Customer Service.

One crucial component of any automated attendant should be the option to press "0" and get a "real" person to help direct your call. No, that doesn't mean that you need to have a dedicated receptionist. If your decision tree is simple enough for your customer to figure out, the "0" option should be used infrequently. So, even if you don't have a dedicated receptionist, when someone presses the "0" key, have a plan to route the call to someone who is most likely to be available. Most automated attendants will also allow you to route to other extensions if the call is not picked up in a certain number of rings. All that means is, if the "0" call gets routed to Sally and she's not there, after a pre-determined number of rings (I suggest a maximum of 3), it automatically gets routed to Joe – you get the idea. It is my hope, naturally, that SOMEONE will be able to pick up the call. If all else fails, you can route the call to a general mailbox. Be sure to have a particular person responsible for checking the general mailbox and responding to any voicemails, either themselves or by making sure the appropriate person gets the message.

Just recently I was calling a government agency to get a copy of a report I had paid for online, but the report had not been automatically delivered. NONE of the options in their automated attendant gave me the option of obtaining the report I was looking for. When I pressed "0" I was told, by a recorded message, that "0" was an invalid option! So, now what do I do?

I listened to the options again and decided to choose the Accounts Receivable Department. Why? Well, I figured that department dealt with money coming in. I was more likely to get a "live" person there.

Sure enough, someone did pick up the phone. I immediately told them that I was not sure whether or not I had the right person and proceeded to explain why I was calling. She didn't know where she should transfer me but, with the receipt number, she could look up the report and email it to me. That's exactly what she did, even though it wasn't really her job. Amazing customer service from someone who could have just said it wasn't her job.

The problem still exists though because, if I have to call back again, I still don't know which option in their decision tree to choose.

How to Answer the Phone

There are a lot of opinions floating around about the correct way to answer a business phone - particularly in a customer service department. They range anywhere from a simple "Yes?" to something syrupy sweet like "Thank you for calling. We're honored to have you as a customer. It's my pleasure to serve you today. How can I help you?".

I don't know about you, but I've been on the receiving end of the "it's my pleasure to serve you", "it's my pleasure to direct your call", etc., etc., etc. And it just starts to annoy me, mostly because it is so obviously not genuine.

I also find it particularly annoying when customer service reps apologize - profusely - for putting me on hold. The more this happens the more I know that they are REQUIRED to say such things. They don't really mean them, but a supervisor might be listening in and they will get hauled up on the carpet if they don't do EXACTLY as they've been instructed.

I'm not sure that the powers-that-be who initiate such rules and regulations have any clue just how annoying they can be to a regular customer.

❖ *Be polite - yes!*

❖ *Be respectful - yes!*

❖ *Be syrupy sweet and disingenuous - NO!*

Don't make the greeting too long.

We've all had to listen to greetings that just seem to go on forever and the people are pretty much out of breath before they finish it. You know what I'm talking about. Something like "Good Morning, this is so-and-so at such-and-such-company or such-and-such-department. It will be my pleasure to serve you today. How may I help you?"

Whew! By the time that's over the customer may have forgotten why they called in the first place.

Some of these greetings even try to squeeze in an ad by telling customers what deals are available - today only! This all just gets to be too much.

My favorite type of greeting assumes that the customer knows which company, and which department they have called. Please, let's not treat them like children.

Here's what I use most of the time: "Good Morning (or Afternoon), this is YOUR NAME." That's it! They already know what company they've called, what department and they're about to tell you why they've called. In addition, they now know who they're talking to. It's a great place to start without annoying a customer with a long, drawn out greeting.

The only change I would make here is if the customer service person is also the receptionist. Then the greeting should be altered slightly to: Good Morning (or Afternoon), YOUR COMPANY, this is YOUR NAME. That's it. Then just be quiet and let the customer speak.

"Personal Anecdote"

I'll never forget one time that I answered the company phone directly when the receptionist was unavailable. I answered it exactly as I have suggested above, Good Morning, NAME OF COMPANY, this is Victoria. And then I waited ... No one said anything. So I ventured a "Hello?"

The person on the other end gave me a startled "What?"

So, I said, "Hello, you've got Victoria. Can I help you?"

"Oh!" came the response, "You mean I've got a REAL person? I was waiting for the options menu to kick in."

This person was expecting an automated attendant and was confused.

After I explained that our company liked to actually answer the phone they agreed that that was a great idea. I was then able to ascertain exactly what they wanted and get them to the correct person immediately. Well, actually, they were looking to talk to me!

Return Voice Messages

This may seem like a straightforward statement. It's pretty self-evident and just common sense, right? Return your voice messages.

However, it has been my experience that most people don't actually return their messages. I'm not quite sure why. If a customer leaves you a message and wants to hear back from you, why wouldn't you return their call?

It has always surprised me - it still does - when I call someone back in response to a message they left for me on voicemail and they sound genuinely surprised, and often very thankful, that I have returned their call.

And, to be honest, I'm genuinely surprised that they are surprised. Of course I returned their call. They took the time to leave me a message. They asked me to call them back. Why wouldn't I call them back?

It is an unfortunate sign of the times when we are surprised when someone does actually call us back.

Don't fall into this kind of apathetic behavior. Always make sure to return any messages left on your answering machine or voicemail.

Telephone Tag

That's not to say that you won't end up playing telephone tag. That happens a lot, too. They got your voicemail and left a message, now you're returning their call only to get their voicemail.

The proper thing to do, of course, is to leave them a message. You definitely want them to know that you returned their call and should say so, nicely, in the message you leave. Something like, "Hi, it's YOUR NAME, returning your call. I'll be in the office the rest of the day. My number is YOUR NUMBER. I look forward to talking with you,"

This is a polite message that reminds the person that they initiated the contact. It's also a good idea to leave your phone number with the message. This is common courtesy so the customer doesn't have to look up your phone number in order to call you back. In my experience I have found that most people appreciate you leaving them your number.

I shouldn't have to say it, but I'm going to. When leaving a message speak slowly and clearly. How many times have you received voice messages that you just can't figure out? They've either said they're name, company name or phone number way too fast, too softly or too garbled for you to figure out. Then you are unable to return their call. Be clear, slow and concise. Your customer will appreciate not having to guess at any part of your message.

It Doesn't Stop There

But, it doesn't stop there. Yes, you have returned your customer's call and, in all likelihood, you feel that your job is done and the ball is in their court. Well, yes - and no.

Don't forget that this is a customer that buys products from your company and that's exactly what you want them to do. So, it's always a good idea to go that extra mile and set a reminder to call them again if you haven't heard from them in a day or so. They called you for some reason and, as you haven't yet spoken with them, you can't be sure what they were calling about.

Perhaps they have solved the problem themselves and that's why they haven't called back but there's no way you can know that for sure.

They may not have been able to decipher your message, they may have accidentally deleted it, they may not have had the time to listen to it or the time to call you back. Any, or all, of these are possible along with a laundry list of other reasons.

Call them again. If you get them in person - great! You can then determine what you can help them with. If you get their voicemail again, leave another message, but this one will be a little different. Say something like, "Hi, it's YOUR NAME, from YOUR COMPANY NAME. I'm just following up to make sure you got my message okay. Please feel free to call me at YOUR PHONE NUMBER."

Follow up is very important and is almost always appreciated by your customer.

Don't Badger

There is a difference between following up and badgering a customer, too. If you don't hear back from them after your second follow-up, then it's probably best to let it go. As long as you have made sure that your message was clear, then, if they don't call you back after two follow-ups, they are likely not going to, and you may never know why.

"Personal Anecdote"

I clearly remember one customer, from a very large and important company, thanking me profusely for returning their call. I told them that it was not only my job, but my pleasure, to return their call. Their response was, "Well, you seem to be the only one that feels that way. I've been trying to get hold of several people today and have left lots of voicemail messages and, so far, you're the only person that's called me back."

This was a large and well known company in the film industry. It absolutely amazes me that this gentleman was having difficulty getting people to return his calls.

❧❤❧

In Chapter 3 we have learned:

✔ *How to determine if you need an automated attendant or a "live" receptionist*

✔ *The importance of setting up an automated attendant correctly*

✔ *How to answer telephone calls correctly*

✔ *The importance of returning voice messages*

CHAPTER 4
COMMUNICATING WITH YOUR CUSTOMERS

In Chapter 4 we'll learn how to communicate effectively in several mediums.

When it comes to excellent customer service, any communication needs to be clear and concise. That includes communicating with your customer:

➤ *In person*

➤ *By email*

➤ *On the telephone*

➤ *By regular mail*

➤ *Upselling (a brief discussion)*

IN PERSON

In-person contact with your customer can be both the easiest and the most difficult. With in-person contact all factors can come into play - your body language, your tone of voice, your attitude, even your appearance.

While all of this is still open to interpretation from your customer, it's often easier to avoid any misunderstandings. However, it's also possible for the customer to realize that you're annoyed, disinterested or uncaring simply by your body language or tone of voice. You can be saying all the right things but conveying something entirely different by the tone you use or with your body language.

In customer service, you need to genuinely want to help your customer, genuinely want to make things right. If you're just going through the motions, your customer will know it, particularly with in-person contact. They may not know how or why they know it, but they will know.

IN PERSON TRUMPS ON THE PHONE

A pet peeve of mine is how some customer service people seem to think that someone on the phone is more important than someone standing right in front of them. How can that be? If someone has actually taken the time to physically show up at a company's place of business to get some help, how can someone who has just picked up a phone have priority? But it happens time and time again and you've probably experienced it yourself. You're at the customer service counter. A customer service rep begins to serve you and then the phone rings. "Just a minute," they say and then pick up the phone and help the person on the phone while you just stand there waiting. I'm sorry, but that's just plain wrong, not to mention rude. The person at the counter has taken the time and effort to actually come to your place of business. They are the priority.

Naturally, that doesn't mean that the person on the phone is not important. Of course they are, they are a customer. However, the person standing right in front of you is the priority.

So, as a customer service rep, what's the best way to handle such as situation?

Option A
Answer the phone, of course. Tell the person that you are currently serving a customer but you'd be happy to call them back just as soon as you're finished. Quickly get their name and phone number and then get back to the person at the counter.

Option B
If there is another customer service rep that is free, ask them to take the call.

Option C
Ask the caller if they would like to be put through to someone else, as you are not able to help them right now because you are serving someone else.

Option D
If you have a voicemail system available, explain to the customer that you are currently helping a customer but you'd be glad to put them through to voicemail and the first available person will call them back.

Certainly you'll get some customers who think you should deal with them immediately. You will need to be polite, but firm. The customer standing right in front of you is the priority. That customer has made a much greater effort than simply picking up the phone and, as such, should be treated with the respect they deserve and should, unquestionably, be the priority. However, you will most likely have to deal with phone customers that believe they should be the priority and don't think they should have to transferred to someone else, wait for a call back or leave a voicemail.

For more ideas on how to deal with such customers see Chapter 5 - Dealing With Different Types of Customers. We'll go over how to handle demanding, unhappy, unreasonable, abusive customers and even accommodating customers.

By Email

Email Formatting, Spelling and Grammar

Let's start with the basics of communicating by email. You need to always - ALWAYS - make sure that any email you send to a customer is properly formatted, that all the words are spelled correctly and that your grammar is also correct.

Nothing screams unprofessional like poor spelling and grammar skills. Formatting is important, too, of course.

Make sure that your spelling and grammar checker are turned on - and don't ignore those red underlines. Now, there is always the chance that what you have written is correct and the checking program is wrong - it does happen. However, it doesn't happen very often. So, be sure to double check and correct any errors BEFORE sending that email.

Formatting correctly makes the email easier to read. Don't make it one long run-on sentence. When faced with something that is difficult to read quickly, the customer may simply give up and hit the delete button.

Any communication you have with your customer should be easy for them to understand.

Email Etiquette

Professional email etiquette can be a little different from personal email etiquette. Although you want to come across as friendly, don't stray into over-familiar. For example, emoticons (smiley faces, etc.) DO NOT belong in emails to your customers. Resist any urge to use them.

Remember, too, that typing in ALL CAPS, conveys that you are SHOUTING to most people. You need to avoid this as well. If you feel you need to emphasize a few words in your email use either bold or italics.

If your customer has initiated the email contact, when you reply, do them the courtesy of including their original request in your reply. In business, people send lots of requests to lots of people. If you simply reply with an answer, they may not remember what the original question was. Don't make them search back through their emails to find out what it was they asked you in the first place. Be pro-active and make things easy for them. It will be appreciated.

The Tone of Your Email

Always be mindful that in any email communications, the tone of any message is applied by the reader, not the writer. All that means, simply put, is that when someone reads your email, they decide what the tone is - conciliatory, belligerent, annoyed, helpful, accusatory - the list is endless.

Remember, in an email the reader can't hear your tone of voice, they can't see your body language, they can't tell if you're smiling or frowning. But what they can do is imagine and they WILL apply that imagination to the email they have received from you.

You can write what you consider to be a perfectly benign email and the reader could interpret it as insulting, condescending or worse. Perhaps they're having a bad day. Maybe a certain word or phrase sets them off. It's hard to say.

So, how do you combat this type of problem?

First of all, in my experience, I've found that most people don't actually read their emails, they scan them. This can lead to all kinds of misunderstandings if they skip some words that are crucial to the correct meaning. And, believe me, that happens all the time and ends up taking several emails to clear things up - if that happens at all.

POINT FORM

I have found that it is best to keep emails as short as possible and, often, in point form. That makes it easy to scan and, the shorter it is, the less chance there exists for a misunderstanding.

ONE ISSUE PER EMAIL

In addition to this, you only want to cover one issue per email. If your customer has separate issues, deal with each one separately and in separate emails. Again, this helps eliminate any misunderstanding and it also makes each email easier for the customer to read and digest.

BY PHONE

YOUR TELEPHONE PERSONA AND "VOICE"

It's true that many of us have a certain persona and voice that we use almost exclusively when we're speaking on the phone. You may not even realize that you do it. I know I certainly didn't until my husband once said to me, "You're using your telephone voice."

What?

Apparently I speak more loudly, more clearly, more slowly and I tend to apply more effort to enunciation when I'm on the phone. Who knew?

And that brings me to the fact that, though some of us do this without thinking, others need to learn this skill.

Telephone communications need to be clear.

TONE OF VOICE

The tone of your voice also contributes a lot to what your customer hears and understands from the conversation. The tone of your voice can indicate many things to your customer.

❖ *If you sound bored, they will assume that you're not interested in helping them.*

❖ *If you sound angry, they will assume you're angry with them. Even if the anger was caused by something else entirely (a fight with your significant other, your boss, a co-worker), they don't know that and will assume it's directed at them.*

❖ *If you seem distracted, they'll assume you just don't care.*

When speaking with a customer, you need to devote all of your attention to the conversation. If you do, it will come across.

SMILE - REALLY!

So, what's the best way to make sure you've got the right tone of voice?

Smile – Really!

It may sound odd, but people can actually "hear" a smile. Why? Because, if you're smiling, you're naturally relaxed and open and engaged. It's practically impossible to sound bored or angry when you're smiling.

This shouldn't be too tough if you like your job and like dealing with your customers.

Sure, we all have bad days, but you need to put that aside when you're on the phone with your customers.

PACING

Pacing your conversation can help with the clarity of what you're saying. If you're speaking too quickly, your customer may miss some of what you're saying. Also, if you're speaking quickly, your customer may feel that they "can't get a word in edgewise". Be sure to pause occasionally so that your customer can ask questions or, at least, join in the conversation. Remember it's supposed to be a conversation, not a lecture.

Likewise, if you speak too slowly you're customer may get bored or think that you're being condescending.

Let you customer's speech pattern help you set the pace.

Listen first, then talk.

VOLUME

Try to make sure that you use enough volume so that you are heard clearly but not so much that it sounds like you're shouting. It's hard to put conversational inflections in your voice when you're speaking too loudly.

On the flip side, if you speak too softly you may find that your customer keeps asking you to repeat things. It's important to note that if they have to ask you to repeat yourself too many times, they are going to get very frustrated.

Try to find a balance.

INFLECTIONS

Your telephone persona also needs to be, for lack of a better word, lively. All that means is that you need to make sure you have inflections in your voice. We've all heard monotone speakers - snore! Listening to someone's monotone voice is great if you need help getting to sleep, but it's not good for clear communications because after a couple of sentences people will get bored and stop listening. Yes, they may still be on the phone so they're still hearing you, but they're not listening. There's a big difference.

SUGGESTION

I know of several people who like to have a mirror on their desk so they can make sure they're smiling when they speak with their customers. It works for them. Personally, looking at myself in a mirror all day kind of freaks me out. But it's certainly worth a try.

I find that getting myself into the right frame of mind for the day works well - most of the time.

I've always liked to say - if you want to be happy, BE HAPPY!

BY REGULAR MAIL

Although it is very rare in today's electronic era, some people do still like to communicate by regular mail.

If you receive communication from your customer in letter format, look for a telephone number and/or an email address. If there is no telephone number or email address available on the letter, then you will need to respond by regular mail.

If there is a phone number, you should call the person for the initial contact. However, you then need to follow-up the phone call with a letter recapping what was discussed during the phone conversation and detailing anything that was agreed upon.

If there is an email address in the letter, it is alright to make initial contact using their email address. You will need to ask them to respond to the email

Common Sense Customer Service

so you can be sure they received it. In this day and age, so many emails get lost in junk filters that you can never be certain the intended recipient actually received your email unless they let you know they did.

Even if they do respond to your email, follow up with a regular letter. It is common courtesy to respond to someone in the manner they have contacted you. In the regular letter you will need to recap what was in your email and the fact that they did respond to your email.

Upselling

In many industries, sales and customer service are inextricably linked, but I'm only going to touch on upselling as a customer service rep, as the sales part of customer service is beyond the scope of this book.

There is nothing wrong with trying to upsell a customer that you are currently dealing with. However, don't badger them. It's a fine line and all too easy to cross.

Yes, they'd probably like to know if there's a better version of the product they want, or an accessory that naturally compliments what they're buying. I know I would. These are good things to know before they complete a purchase.

However, if the customer says they don't want it, or don't want to hear about all the additional stuff, then STOP! If you're too aggressive it's possible to lose the initial sale as well. Tread softly.

Unfortunately, a lot of Internet marketers don't seem to learn this lesson very well. We've all experienced it. We agree to purchase something that we actually want and all we want to do is pay for it and get what we paid for. But it seems that, at times, you have to go through an endless parade of upsells, and downsells, before they even let you get to the point where you can get what you wanted in the first place. If it's several of these in a row it often results in abandoned carts and they don't get the initial sale at all.

This applies to in-person sales, too. Yes, be helpful, but also learn how to read your customer. Both body language and tone of voice will tell you if the customer is getting frustrated or annoyed. If you see these warning signs, it's time to stop "selling" the customer and just let them buy.

In Chapter 4 we have learned how to communicate effectively in several mediums

✔ *In person*

✔ *By email*

✔ *On the phone*

✔ *By regular mail*

✔ *Clear and concise communications are required in any medium*

✔ *Upselling is also a form of communication as long as it doesn't cross over into badgering*

CHAPTER 5
DEALING WITH DIFFERENT TYPES OF CUSTOMERS

In Chapter 5 we'll learn how to deal with different types of customers.

First we'll start with understanding just what your customer's needs are.

Then, we'll move on to the types of customer you're likely to encounter:

➤ *The demanding customer*

➤ *The unhappy customer*

➤ *The unreasonable customer*

➤ *The abusive customer*

➤ *The accommodating customer*

➤ *Internal customers*

UNDERSTANDING YOUR CUSTOMERS

ACCENTUATE THE POSITIVE
Just like the famous Johnny Mercer/Harold Arlen song says:

> *You've got to accentuate the positive*
>
> *Eliminate the negative*
>
> *Latch on to the affirmative*
>
> *Don't mess with Mister In-Between*

You can find all the lyrics and history on Wikipedia

http://en.wikipedia.org/wiki/Ac-Cent-Tchu-Ate_the_Positive

And several videos on YouTube

http://www.youtube.com/watch?v=f3jdbFOidds

A positive attitude is very, very important when dealing with ANY customer. Let me say that again - a positive attitude is very, very important when dealing with any customer.

When you exude positivity, it's hard for people to be negative because of the encouraging atmosphere it creates. People become more enthusiastic, more hopeful and more reasonable in such an atmosphere.

Here's a couple of examples of how to generate that kind of atmosphere with just a few words:

Instead of simply saying "no" to someone's request, try saying, "Let me see what I can do."

If you don't have the authority to make a decision, then don't automatically tell the customer you can't do anything. Tell them you'll see what you can do. Explain to them that you have to talk to someone with the authority to make such a decision. Tell them when you'll be doing this and when you'll get back to them. And ... don't forget to follow up (see Chapter 6 on promises and follow up).

Another approach is - instead of telling a customer you can't do what they want, tell them what you CAN do for them.

Customers can be very understanding and may realize, before you even say anything, that they can't get everything they want. But if you tell them what you can do, rather than what you can't do, you'll create a more positive atmosphere and will, most likely, get a more positive response.

Important Note: Be sure you know the limits of your authority before you promise a customer anything. You don't want to be put in the position of having to retract an offer you've made to a customer because you've overstepped your bounds. That quickly turns a happy customer into an irate customer.

Note to Managers: See Chapter 11 about empowering your employees.

WHAT DO MOST CUSTOMERS REALLY WANT?

❖ *To feel valued*

❖ *To feel listened to*

❖ *To have confidence that their concerns will be addressed*

❖ *To be treated with respect*

Most customers just want to know that they are actually being heard. They want to be sure their concerns, problems and/or questions will be addressed. They want to know what their options are. They need to know they are valued. And, as a customer service person, you need to show them that they are valued as a customer and that, when they have a valid concern or complaint, it will be dealt with quickly and fairly.

Learn to Listen

It seems to me that, in an effort to keep control of the situation and to resolve things, a lot of customer service reps just keep talking. If you find yourself doing this - it can be caused by nervousness as well - take a deep breath and be quiet for a few seconds. If you're customer doesn't take advantage of the lull to express his or her concerns, then ask a question, be quiet and wait for their response. Even after you think they have stopped talking, wait a couple seconds more, they may still have something else to say.

Recap

Once you are sure they have finished, repeat back to them what you think it is they have said, what they want, what they need.

This should be a recap or a précis of what they just said and not just a parroting back. You can say something like, "Okay. What I understand your concern - or your request - or your complaint - to be is ..."

Now, if you were actually listening, this should not be difficult. If your mind wandered off because you were disinterested, this is going to be tough. You need to be fully present when you are listening.

Doing this recap accomplishes two things:

❖ *It makes sure that both you and the customer understand the concern*

❖ *It makes the customer feel listened to and respected*

This should get you off to a good start, with both you and your customer working towards an equitable solution.

The Golden Rule

As a customer service representative, a good rule of thumb is to treat someone the way you would like to be treated. Yes, this sounds just like the old adage "Do unto others as you would have them do unto you." The saying has been around for a very, very long time for a very, very good reason. It is, quite simply, common sense. If you are able to put yourself in the other person's shoes, then you are more likely to be sympathetic to their needs.

Now, much as we would all like things to go smoothly, that is, unfortunately, not always the case. You will, without a doubt, run into difficult, unreasonable and even abusive customers. There are ways to handle all of these types of customers and they are covered in the following sections of this chapter.

THE DEMANDING CUSTOMER

A demanding customer can be very vocal. You may find them raising their voice if you are on the phone with them. In person they can cause quite a disruption. Even emails from such a customer can come across as vocal and you just might find the message has a lot of words in ALL CAPS in their effort to get their dissatisfaction across.

Frequently, a demanding customer doesn't really care what you need to do or how things are supposed to work. They simply want a solution and they want it NOW!

Just as frequently, they often aren't inclined to answer any questions you may ask in an effort to discern the problem or find a solution.

In essence, demanding customers are also impatient customers. You're expected not only to know what the problem is but to immediately solve it, with virtually no input.

UNDERSTANDING THE PROBLEM

Even though the customer may not like it, they will need to help you understand the problem in order for you to be able to find an equitable solution. So, like it or not, you've got to ask the demanding customer questions to be able to help them.

REMAIN CALM

In order to deal with this kind of customer you're going to need to be calm and steady. Don't let the customer fluster you. Don't let their false sense of urgency push you into reacting too quickly or promising something you shouldn't.

And, above all, don't display any frustration. Sure, they'll vent their frustration, but you need to stay calm (and, trust me, I know how difficult this can be). You may even have to repeat your questions several times in order to make them understand that they need to answer them.

Try to keep the same calm and steady tone each time you ask a question (even if it's for the third or fourth time). I know it's hard to keep the frustration from your voice and/or your body language, but that's what you need to do. It may help to think of it like an adult explaining to a child. No, I am not suggesting for one minute that you actually treat the customer like a child, just that you need to be as patient as you would be with a child.

If, for example, you let out a heavy sigh before asking the same question for the umpteenth time, the customer will now know that you're frustrated and they'll assume you are not going to be helpful.

Don't Get Intimidated

A demanding customer will try to take advantage of any perceived weakness on your part. If you get flustered or stumble over your words they'll try to take advantage of the situation. Remain calm.

State Clearly What You Can Do

As mentioned earlier, once you are able to discern the customer's concern, recap the problem as you see it, try to get their agreement on the issue. then state, clearly, what you can do.

Last Resort

There may be times when you just can't get a demanding customer to listen to reason. In cases such as this you have a couple of options:

❖ *Tell them calmly that, unless they can answer your questions, you will not be able to help them.*

❖ *Give them the option of speaking to a supervisor.*

The Unhappy Customer

Almost everything that applies to a demanding customer, applies to an unhappy customer, with a few minor differences.

Unhappy customers are more likely to answer your questions so that you can reach a solution. Usually the unhappy customer is all too eager to tell you why they are unhappy. Although it may not seem like it at the time, this is a gift.

Sorting Out What's Important

As the customer vents their frustration, listen carefully for the key reasons for their unhappiness. Sometimes it's hard to break into the conversation with an unhappy customer, but you need to try. Never raise your voice, though, and never, never get into a shouting match with a customer.

You may find that if you speak softly in situations like this, they'll have to stop and really listen so they can understand what you're saying.

Once they are listening, recap what you think are the important points and try to get their agreement on the key points.

Proceed To The Solution

It's a good thing to know that inside every unhappy customer, there is a happy customer striving to get out.

As soon as they realize they are valued and being listened to, they will readily work with you towards a solution and are often quite reasonable about the outcome.

The Unreasonable Customer

It's true, sometimes there is just no pleasing someone.

You will, at some point in your career, come across someone that is totally unreasonable. And, you may be surprised to discover, they often KNOW they are being unreasonable.

Sometimes they're just "trying you on for size" but, more often than not, they have decided that the only way to get what they want, or what they think they deserve, it to be totally over the top with their attitude.

There will come a time that, after trying your best to appease or accommodate a customer, you may have to resign yourself to the fact that you cannot give them what they want and that may mean losing a customer.

You'll simply have to tell them that, while you would love to help them, you simply can't give them what they want. You can tell them that they can certainly speak to a supervisor, or the owner, but the outcome will be the same.

Important Note: In a good company, where employees are well versed on company policy, this kind of statement should be backed up by their supervisor or the owner of the company.

Be Careful Who You Label Unreasonable

Truly unreasonable customers are rare, so don't start labeling too many customers as "unreasonable" or you may end up with no customers.

The Abusive Customer

I'm afraid that I don't have much time for abusive customers. There is simply no justification for such a thing.

Yes, I understand that they are unhappy, but that does not give them the right to abuse another person.

Over the Phone

I have a fairly simple rule for dealing with an abusive person over the phone. If they resort to offensive language (swearing, etc.), tell them simply, calmly and politely that their language is offensive. You will do what you can to help but if they continue to use such language you will have no choice but to end the call. If they continue, do not say another thing - hang up. That's right, I just told you to hang up on a customer! No one has the right to abuse you no matter how upset they are - **PERIOD**.

You're next step, and a very important one, is to immediately tell your supervisor what you did and why. You want to be sure that if the abusive person calls back and wants to speak with your boss that he or she is aware of what took place. A good supervisor will support you.

IN AN EMAIL

If you receive an abusive email, do not respond to it. Tell your supervisor about it, send them a copy and let them deal with the customer.

IN PERSON

Dealing with an abusive customer in person can be pretty scary. There may even be times when you are concerned about your physical safety. It's best to remove yourself from this kind of situation as quickly as possible.

If a customer becomes abusive, ask them calmly and firmly to stop. If they do not, immediately call for your supervisor.

If you are concerned about your physical safety, immediately call security. If your company does not have a security department, call 911.

If the personal is physically abusive - make a lot of noise. This may scare them off. Try to remember what the person looked like so you can give a description to the police if you need to.

If making noise doesn't scare them off, get away as quickly as you can to a safe location or to a place where you can get help.

Nothing is worth risking your personal safety - nothing!

THE ACCOMMODATING CUSTOMER

ACCOMMODATING CUSTOMERS ARE GOLD!

Let's not forget the amazing customer who truly wants to work with you and will do just about anything to avoid upsetting you. Don't take these customers for granted. They are a gift and should be treated as such.

That being said, if you marginalize these customers and only do the minimum expected, or worse yet - nothing at all! - then your gift of such an amazing customer will probably turn into one of the customers you'd really rather not deal with.

You need to let these customers know just how much they are appreciated. They make your job easy - tell them so. They brighten your day - tell them so.

Then, reach an equitable solution with them and make sure that you follow through on anything you have promised.

We all want more of these customers and they better job we do as customer service people, the more of these customers we're likely to have.

Internal Customers

What Are Internal Customers?

Simply put, your internal customers are your fellow employees.

A company, in essence, is a community of people all working towards the same goal. So, if your fellow employees require your assistance, treat them just as well as you would treat your customers.

Don't Play Politics

I've seen it happen in many companies where individuals try to jostle for position. Some employees will undermine, or even lie about, other employees to advance their own agenda.

In most cases, the supervisors are wise enough to see such machinations, but not always.

In any case, don't be drawn into such behavior. Simply refuse to play!

If you do your job well and treat both your internal and external customers well, it will get noticed. Shine by your own accomplishments, not by undermining someone else's.

In Chapter 5 we have learned

✔ *How to understand your customer's needs and motivations.*

✔ *How to effectively deal with different types of customers:*

- *The demanding customer*
- *The unhappy customer*
- *The unreasonable customer*
- *The abusive customer*
- *The accommodating customer*
- *Internal customers*

Chapter 6

Under-promise and over-deliver
or
How to be a hero to your customer

In Chapter 6 we'll learn:

➤ *How to make realistic promises*

➤ *How to keep the customer informed of any changes or delays*

➤ *How to effectively follow up on any promises that have been made*

Promises, Promises, Promises

"Now a promise made is a debt unpaid"

The Cremation of Sam McGee, Robert W. Service

http://www.poetryfoundation.org/poem/174348

These are true words from poet Robert W. Service. When you make a promise it doesn't end there. The debt incurred by any promise is not discharged until that promise is kept.

Don't make promises lightly and never, ever make a promise you can't possibly hope to keep just to make a customer happy. When that customer discovers that you either didn't have the ability, or the intention, of keeping your promise, well, you've just lost a customer. You might also put your job at risk if the customer decides to complain - particularly if it happens to more than one customer.

If you want to be seen as a hero to your customer (and who doesn't), you need to make sure that when you promise them something that you are able to keep that promise. Better still, if you are able to keep your promise in a timely manner then you will have a truly grateful and suitably impressed customer.

The key to this is not to promise anything that you can't deliver. That goes for such things as delivery promises, too. Don't tell someone they can have something in a day just to keep them happy when you know it will take 2-3 days, at least. That's just setting the customer up for disappointment and making you look unreliable or untruthful.

Under Promise and Over Deliver

The best thing you can do for your customer is to give them reasonable and accurate promises. Yes, they may be unhappy that something they want right now won't be available for a couple of days, however, if you tell them you can have it for them in 3 days, and then deliver it in 2 days, you're a hero! But, if you tell them you can have it for them in 2 days and then deliver it in 3 days, you're a zero.

No, I am not suggesting that you "pad" the truth. But, as we all know, things don't always go according to plan. It's best, if some factors are totally out of your control, to give the customer a reasonable estimate. And, tell them you're giving them an estimate. Tell them that, according to your experience and knowledge, the time frame you have quoted them is the most accurate one you can give them.

Keeping the Customer Informed

If, for some reason, the estimate you have given a customer will not be met - tell them as soon as you know. Don't wait for them to call you to say their item hasn't arrived as promised. Head it off at the pass and contact them with an update. Naturally, they will be disappointed, but certainly not as disappointed as they would be if you hadn't told them about the delay at all.

This applies to anything that affects any promise you have made, not just delivery dates. If a credit you promised gets delayed, tell your customer and tell them why. If you promised them an answer to their inquiry on a certain date and discover that you won't have the necessary information, tell them about the delay, the reason for the delay and give them an updated estimate of the date you will have the information they need.

Follow Up, Follow Up, Follow Up

Follow up with anyone that has given you a promise that affects your customer. You may have been told that the item your customer wants will be shipped on a certain day. If the actual shipping of the product is out of your control, then follow up with whoever is responsible for meeting the promised shipping date. Don't rely on that person to let you know if there's a problem. You need to be pro-active. If there is a delay in shipping you need to know. That gives you the opportunity to contact your customer and tell them about the delay and give them the current estimate.

Follow up with anyone who has been tasked with the responsibility of fulfilling a promise you made to a customer. There are many situations in which you will be able to promise a customer something but then have to delegate that responsibility to someone else to fulfill the promise. Be sure to follow up with that person to make sure they are still on schedule.

Follow up with your customer to make sure they have received the promised item and that they are satisfied.

Following up and keeping your customer informed shows them that you respect and appreciate them.

See Chapter 9 - Good Note Keeping - for ways to make sure you don't forget to follow up.

In Chapter 6 we have learned

✔ *Accurate, realistic promises are always best*

✔ *Keeping the customer informed for any delays or changes is always the best way to head off any disappoint or problems*

✔ *Following up is key to retaining a customer and keeping them happy*

Chapter 7
Knowing your limits

In Chapter 7 we'll learn about the importance of knowing your limits. It's great to be empowered but it brings responsibility along with it.

So, it's imperative that we learn:

➤ *Why it's important to know, and understand, any company policies that affect you and/or your customer*

➤ *Why it's important to understand your limits and stick to them.*

Company Policies

Make sure that you are aware of any company policies that will affect your ability to serve your customer - good, bad or indifferent.

Many companies have policies concerning returns, refunds, markdowns, credits and more. Be sure you get a written copy of any such policies and make sure you know how they relate to your ability to do your job. If in doubt, ask for clarification.

Be sure to be aware of any company policies regarding:

❖ *When and how to issue a refund*

❖ *When and how to issue a credit*

❖ *When returns are acceptable and when they're not*

❖ *When you can offer free shipping and to whom*

❖ *When you can offer expedited service and to whom*

❖ *When discounts are allowed and to whom*

❖ *What kind of discounts are allowed*

- *A percentage of the original price*
- *A percentage of the sale price*
- *A dollar amount*

❖ *When it's acceptable to give away free samples*

❖ *Whether there is special pricing for particular customers, such as educational or non-profit institutions*

I have worked with many companies that have preferred customers who receive special pricing. I have also worked with companies that do their best to support non-profit organizations by either giving them product or allowing them to buy it at a significantly reduced price. Usually, there is a procedure in place to verify that the company and/or institution meet certain criteria to qualify for such consideration. Make sure you're aware of any procedure that your company has to ascertain the eligibility for such discounts or giveaways.

Your company may have more – or fewer – policies than those mentioned here. The key point is – be up-to-date on all of the company's policies that can affect your customer and how you do your job.

"Personal Anecdote"

A good example of great customer service, through empowered employees who understand company policies, was an encounter I had just recently with the world's largest online retailer – yes, Amazon.

I had purchased some tax software that, no matter what I did, simply would not download. That left me faced with having to go directly to the software manufacturer to purchase it at $30 more than the price on Amazon.

I spoke with customer service several times and they tried their best to correct the download problem, but could not come up with a solution. So, I did purchase it from the software manufacturer and it downloaded just fine.

So, what did Amazon do? Well, first off, they credited me for the purchase (something that is not normally done for software) and then the customer service person said that, because I had to pay more for it elsewhere, they would put a credit on my account for the extra $30 I had to spend.

Yes, Amazon knows customer service!

Use Your Authority Wisely

Some companies are comfortable with empowering their employees, within certain limits. If your company is one that has empowered you, be sure to treat such authority with great respect.

Be sure to apply common sense judgment when using the authority you have. You don't want to be giving away discounts and credits unless it is actually necessary. Don't forget that such a thing affects your company's bottom line. Prices are set where they are for a good reason. Your employer needs to make a reasonable profit. You may not realize it, but every item sold needs to contain a certain amount of profit in order to:

- ❖ *Pay the wholesale price of the item*

- ❖ *Pay for the rent and/or mortgage on the building*

- ❖ *Pay for heating, lights and repairs*

- ❖ *Pay for taxes and insurance*

- ❖ *Re-invest in the company*

- ❖ *And, most importantly, pay your salary*

So, don't be too quick to "give away the farm" in order to make your customers happy. Reserve your trusted authority to times when it is really needed and it really matters.

In Chapter 7 we have learned

✔ *Why it's important to be fully versed in all of your company's policies*

✔ *Why it's important to respect the trust a company places in you when they empower you to make certain decisions.*

CHAPTER 8
DEALING WITH STRESS

In Chapter 8 we'll learn:

➤ *Stress is something that comes with the job*

➤ *Why it's important to learn how to deal with the stress*

➤ *When to ask for help*

DON'T TAKE IT PERSONALLY

In most cases, a customer doesn't want to upset you, they are simply frustrated. If they get upset, or even abusive, don't take it personally. However, if you are exposed to an abusive customer - refer to "the abusive customer" in Chapter 5.

Now, I know from personal experience that advising you to "not take it personally" is a very easy thing to say and a very difficult thing to do in actual practice. Yes, I've had my fair share of teeth-grinding, tongue-biting and even more tears than I care to admit to.

Absolutely, at times, you'll need to blow off some steam. The key here is to do it privately and never, ever in front of a customer. You shouldn't do it in front of your boss or co-workers, either, although sometimes that's a little harder to avoid.

ON THE PHONE

There have been many, many times when I've called a customer a jerk, or worse. GASP! But, that has ALWAYS been AFTER I've hung up the phone. It's a perfect time to allow yourself a little release from a stressful situation. The customer has seen you as professional and helpful and, after you hang up, you get the opportunity to express your opinion and relieve some stress.

One key thing to remember here is - make ABSOLUTELY certain you have cut the telephone connection before your outburst. We've all heard the horror stories of people thinking they have hung up the phone only to find the customer is still on the line and has heard every word of their stress-relieving rant! Don't let this happen to you.

IN PERSON

It's a little tougher to contain your frustration with a customer when you are dealing with them in person. But you need to do it in order to remain professional.

Common Sense Customer Service

Maintain your cool until the customer leaves. Find an empty room, close the door and go ahead and vent, but watch the volume. Odds are that the room you have chosen is not sound proof.

I knew someone who had a small stuffed animal that was made, apparently, precisely for the purpose of venting your frustrations. It was made to throw against a wall - really. But, no matter how you threw it, it would always end up sitting on its butt and smiling at you. It was hard not to smile, or even laugh, when that happened and then there went the frustration and stress.

But it's also a good idea that, if you do feel you need to throw something, make sure it's not breakable. I'm just sayin'.

If It's Truly Too Much

If the stress you're feeling is truly overwhelming, you need to do something about it before it causes health issues.

Speak with your boss and perhaps they can help you deal with it. Perhaps you can stop dealing directly with customers for a while. Perhaps your company will pay for some stress-relieving classes like yoga or meditation. Or, if the situation warrants, perhaps you'll need to seek professional help.

If the stress continues to overwhelm you, you need to ask yourself if this is the field you actually want to be in. Customer service is not for everyone and there's no shame in admitting it's not for you.

If you find that that is the case, it's time to start looking for a career in a different field. Try to decide what it is you want to do, what will make you happy. Take evening courses, if necessary, to get the expertise you need to change fields.

No job is worth feeling stressed constantly.

"Personal Anecdote"

I once experienced being on the listening end of someone ranting about a customer after they had hung up. However, they had two separate phones in their office and they had not put me on hold. They had just laid the phone down on their desk. So I heard their rant about the customer they had just been speaking with.

When he got back on the phone with me I thought it best not to let on that I had heard the rant. After all, I totally understood about such things. He did the right thing. The customer that had so frustrated him had not heard a single word of the rant.

However, it did give me pause and made me wonder what he was saying after he got off the phone with me!

Like I said before, be sure you're not going to be overheard when you break into your stress-relieving rants.

NEVER COMPLAIN TO A CUSTOMER

No matter how much you are tempted, never, ever complain to a customer - about anything.

Your customer is not there to provide moral support for you. They are your customer. You need to vent any frustrations and relieve any stress out of sight and earshot of any customer.

That means that you should never complain to your customers about your job, about the company or their policies, about any of the company's products - you get the idea.

If you do have a problem with your job, your co-workers or any company policies, you need to speak with your boss - privately. And, if your problem is with your boss, and you've tried to resolve it, you need to speak with their boss.

Don't let the stress get out of hand and affect both your professional and personal life. If you find yourself being overwhelmed, you need to deal with the stress constructively and truthfully.

In Chapter 8 we have learned.

✔ *A certain amount of stress comes with the job*

✔ *Dealing with stress, in a constructive manner, is important*

✔ *Getting help when you need it is essential*

CHAPTER 9
GOOD NOTE KEEPING

In Chapter 9 we'll learn the importance of accurate note keeping and explore two methods:

➤ *Manual note keeping*

➤ *Electronic note keeping*

➤ *We'll also learn about the importance of keeping good customer records.*

MANUAL NOTE KEEPING

One of the simplest ways that I have found for manual note keeping is a steno pad. You know the kind I mean, lined pages contained in a book-like format that is spiral bound, usually at the top, however, I have seen some that were spiral bound at the side - either type will do.

No matter what type of notepad you choose, make sure it's in some kind of book format. Notes made on separate pieces of paper, or even sticky notes, just won't work.

Note: Sticky notes do have their place, but not for any notes you may need to reference at a later date. They're great for things that need to be taken care of immediately. However, I had one co-worker that used sticky notes for everything. He'd have a huge number of them pasted to his wall, his desk and his computer screen. If that's the case, then none of them are doing their job. The sense of urgency they should convey gets lost if there are so many of them that you can't possibly deal with them quickly.

BE CONCISE, NOT CRYPTIC

When taking manual notes it's often easy to slip into a type of personal shorthand. While that may work sometimes, you need to be aware that there will be times that others may have to refer to your notes. And, they may have to do that when you're not there (on vacation, off sick). Clear, concise notes can help them deal with a customer effectively during your absence.

Also, if you make your notes too cryptic, will you even be able to decipher them a few weeks, or months, later?

Be Consistent

The key to good record/note keeping is to be consistent. You'll be surprised at how often you'll refer back to your notes, for various reasons. Consistency makes it easier to do that.

When keeping notes manually, my favorite way to start each day is with a fresh page, with the date at the top of the page and with the date highlighted. Highlighting the date makes it easy to see where each day starts and/or ends. Pick a favorite color of highlighter and stick with it. (My personal favorite is neon pink - but that's just me.)

Critical Information

Some critical information that each note should contain are things like:

❖ *The name of the person you were speaking with*

❖ *Their phone and/or extension number*

❖ *The company name*

❖ *Any promises made*

❖ *Any concerns to be addressed*

❖ *Items ordered (unless they were entered into your order system - then the order number, or purchase order number, should be sufficient)*

Separating Notes

It's important to know where one note stops and the next one starts. This can be easily accomplished by either leaving a large space between notes or drawing a horizontal line across the page at the end of each note.

Personally, I like to do both. Why? Well, often, if I need to refer back to a note, I may need to add a little more information. Having extra space to include additional information helps keep the note clear and uncluttered.

Important Note: If you do add to the original note, be sure to include the date the extra information was added.

Indicating Completion

Things can get a little overwhelming and a tad confusing if you don't know which items in your list of notes have been dealt with and which ones still require attention.

Once again, for me, anyway, it's highlighter to the rescue. And, as I also like color-coding, I use a different color of highlighter to indicate which notes have been completed.

When a note I have made has been resolved, I swipe a diagonal line of green highlighter across it to indicate that it is complete. I like to use a transparent highlighter because I still want the entire note to be legible. You never know when you may have to refer back to a note that you thought was over and done with. If you do have to, you want to make sure you can easily read it.

Tracking Older Notes That Are Not Yet Complete

Although keeping all your manual notes together in a book is a good idea, sometimes it becomes difficult, without flipping through a bunch of pages, to determine if there are any notes that still require your attention. After all, once you turn the page on older notes, they are out of sight and, therefore, out of mind.

Here's where sticky notes can play a useful role. Before turning the page, if any of the notes are not complete, place a sticky note on them that sticks out past the side of the page. This makes an easy visual representation of notes that still need your attention.

A little extra: If you like, you can even write a short note on the sticky note that gives some indication of the note that is waiting to be completed.

Keeping Older Books of Notes Handy

Depending on the number of notes you take, you may go through several books. It's a good idea to keep at least a couple of months worth of books at hand for quick reference.

Another good idea is to label the front of each book with the first and last dates that the book includes, again, for easy reference.

"Personal Anecdote"

I once had the dubious pleasure of dealing with customer service people at a small utilities company. As I was sitting at their desk explaining my problem I suggested they take down my phone number so they could call me back with the results. The person reluctantly wrote down my name and phone number on a small piece of scrap paper and then tucked it into their desk blotter. It was all I could do not to shudder at such a sloppy method of note keeping.

Needless to say, I never got a call back and my concern didn't get resolved. I had to go through the whole process again, and then again, with another person, and then, finally, with the manager, before anything got done.

I can't say if this was a result of poor note keeping or just indifference, but the method of note keeping certainly didn't help.

Electronic Note Keeping

There a many programs out there that will allow you to keep electronic notes and that will also remind you to follow up and will allow you to mark any notes as completed.

For larger companies, it's best if the note keeping software is networked, so that anyone dealing with a particular customer can see notes made by anyone else.

In smaller companies, sometimes a standalone software product is all that is needed.

I don't intend to review any particular software product for this purpose, however, here's the minimum you should look for:

❖ *The software should record the user name, time and date when each note is created or edited*

❖ *It should allow for follow up reminders*

❖ *It should have robust search capabilities so you can search all of the notes using various criteria*

❖ *It should be compatible with any contact management software your company uses. Or, be sure that your contact management software has effective note keeping built in.*

❖ *It should ensure that any reminders you set can't be dismissed until the notes are marked as complete.*

Caveat: Any note-keeping software is only as good as the information entered into it. Be sure to learn the software well in order to use it effectively.

Keeping Good Customer Records

Your Customers ARE Your Business

Return customers are always a company's bread and butter. I'm sure everyone has heard how it costs much less to retain a customer than it does to attract a new one. Customer attraction and/or retention is beyond the scope of this book, however, the idea of keeping good records on your customers is certainly part of good customer service.

So, what type of information should you keep on your customers? Here's a few suggestions:

NAME

First and last name are good, but definitely their first name. People like hearing their own name, so if you are dealing with a customer, and you know their name, use it.

EMAIL ADDRESS

A lot of communication is done by email now. If your customer has trusted you with their email address, you need to protect and respect that trust. Never SPAM your customer - never!

ADDRESS AND PHONE NUMBER

If you're shipping to a customer, you will most likely have their address and phone number. Once again, you need to protect such information.

If your company sends out reminders in the mail, then this information will certainly be handy. Once again, don't SPAM.

PREVIOUS PURCHASES

Having a record of your customer's previous purchases can be helpful in many ways. If they have questions or complaints about something they have purchased then you can verify that purchase without the customer having to find the original receipt. Trust me, they will appreciate that.

In addition to that, by reviewing previous purchases you will be able to suggest other items to your customer that they may be interested in.

If at all possible, try to have any customer information you have available when you are speaking with the customer. They will be happy that you remember them.

"PERSONAL ANECDOTE"

When I was working with a very young, dynamic software company I got really excited about the amazing products they were creating. In my excitement, I'm afraid I got a little carried away with telling my customers, by email, all the new and wonderful things that were happening and the new products that were available. I crossed the line and sent emails way too frequently.

I saw my efforts as keeping in touch, which I certainly like to do, and being informative. However, many of my customers, so I found out, thought it was too much.

I was lucky enough to have one wonderful customer who actually took the time to contact me and let me know I had crossed the line. He was very sweet about it. He told me that while he loved hearing from me, however, getting emails about the company and their products more than once a month was excessive. I had started sending my emails once a week and a couple of times I had sent two in one week.

Needless to say, when I was emailing that frequently I got a lot of unsubscribe requests. When I dropped it back to once a month, I got a much more positive response to each email.

Sometimes less actually is more!

PS My heartfelt thanks to that wonderful customer for such constructive criticism.

In Chapter 9 we have learned:

✔ Why it makes sense to keep accurate, concise and legible notes whether you keep the notes manually or electronically

✔ Why we need to set up reminders for any notes that are not yet complete and will require follow up

✔ Why it's important to keep accurate records on each of our customers

CHAPTER 10
FOLLOW UP, FOLLOW UP, FOLLOW UP

In Chapter 10 we'll learn more about the importance of following up.

Even though we have covered the idea of always following up with the customer earlier in this book, it bears repeating and in Chapter 10 we're going to go more in depth about why it is so important.

Communication is key in keeping the customer informed and following up is a great way to communicate.

In this chapter we'll learn:

➤ *Why it's important to follow up*

➤ *How and why you need to keep your customer in the loop*

➤ *The best ways to follow up*

THE IMPORTANCE OF FOLLOWING UP

Although you may be on top of whatever you have promised your customer, being sure that things happen when they need to happen, the customer doesn't know that unless you tell them.

You need to communicate what's happening even if things are on track and particularly if things "go off the rails".

KEEPING YOUR CUSTOMER IN THE LOOP

All this really means is that you need to keep your customer in the loop. They'll appreciate knowing if things are progressing as planned.

They will also appreciate knowing about any delays. They may not LIKE the delays but they will appreciate being informed about them.

You never know, they may have to make some adjustments on their end if what they're expecting from you is delayed. It could affect promises they have made to their customers. You just don't know. And, because you don't know, keeping your customer in the loop is always the best policy.

Why Following Up With Your Customer Is So Important

I know that sometimes it seems like a pain to have to remember to follow up with your customer, even if things are on track. However, you may not know that when you do this it tells a customer many things:

❖ *That they have not been forgotten*

❖ *That they can trust you to give them accurate updates*

❖ *That they can rely on you to be truthful and above board in your dealings with them*

Ways To Follow Up

The most convenient way to follow up with your customer is often by email. In my opinion, this is the best way, too. Why? Because it gives both you and your customer a written record of the update. Also, you can send an email at any time of day that's most convenient for you and your customer can read the email when it's convenient for them. It's another win-win.

However, if the update is urgent, nothing beats the personal touch of a phone call. Pick up the phone and tell the customer if something has happened that will adversely affect any promise you have made.

Whether you speak with them in person, or have to leave a message on their voicemail, always follow up with an email as well. Once again, this gives both of you a written record of the update.

Additional Advantages of Keeping Your Customers Informed

If you get into the habit of keeping your customers informed then you'll have happy, repeat customers who will likely recommend your company to others as well.

Repeat customers are essential to any business.

❧❤❧

In Chapter 10 we have learned

✔ Keeping your customers "in the loop" is good for both the customer and your company – it's a win-win.

✔ Having a written record of any updates, generally by email, is also good for both parties – another win-win

CHAPTER 11
BONUS CHAPTER FOR THE MANAGER/OWNER

Chapter 11 is a bonus chapter written specifically for managers/owners.

In chapter 11 you'll learn:

➤ *Why it's important to lead by example*

➤ *Why technology is important*

➤ *Why you should empower your employees*

➤ *Effective ways to reward your employees (no, it's not always with a raise)*

➤ *Why it's important to praise your employees in public, but to criticize in private*

LEAD BY EXAMPLE

The most powerful thing you can do to inspire your employees is to lead by example. Let them see how you interact fairly, not only with customers, but with employees as well.

Don't fall into the trap of "do as I say, not as I do". If you want them to do the right thing - show them how it's done. Be mindful that your employees will look to you as the example of what's expected of them.

MANAGEMENT BY WALKING AROUND

I once had the opportunity to meet Canadian Major-General Lewis MacKenzie. In 1992 he was the commander of Sector Sarajevo as part of the United Nations Protection Force in the former Yugoslavia. You can read more about him on Wikipedia by just searching on Lewis MacKenzie.

http://en.wikipedia.org/wiki/Lewis_Mackenzie

I'm not quite sure how we got on the subject, but he said that he was a big proponent of "management by walking around". I believe what he meant, in his circumstances, were for the troops to not only be able to see him but to have access to him. He wasn't some far off leader in an ivory tower. He was visible and accessible to his troops.

That's the kind of manager you should strive to be - visible and accessible.

I'm not talking about looking over your employee's shoulder while they are working. That will only make them uncomfortable and, quite possibly, less productive. But, let them know that you are interested and available.

Trust me, the person that knows the job best is the person doing it. Trust your employees to do an exceptional job and, most often, because they know they have your trust and your confidence, they will do an exceptional job.

Be there for them when they need you. Let them know you have their backs. You will be rewarded with loyal, confident and competent employees.

TECHNOLOGY

While it is not my intention to suggest or recommend any particular technology, you do need to arm your employees with the technology they need to do their jobs effectively and efficiently.

To ensure the company and your employees have the right tools, make it a priority to research such things as:

❖ *A good telephone and voicemail system*

❖ *The best computers for the job - Mac, PC, mini-mainframe, mainframe, etc.*

❖ *The best software for the job - off-the-shelf or custom*

❖ *The best email client for your employees to use*

Tip: use a consistent method of creating email addresses so that customers will be able to remember them easily if necessary. Some examples are john. doe@yourcompany.com or, to be very informal, john@yourcompany.com. Also have some generic email addresses like customerservice@yourcompany. com or accountsreceivable@yourcompany.com.

A special note for the generic email addresses: be sure to assign the responsibility for these email addresses to a specific person for better accountability.

OTHER THINGS TO CONSIDER ARE

Auto-attendants - if you have decided to go the auto-attendant route, either as your first line of contact or as a back-up, be sure that the system you choose meets your company's current needs and leaves room for future expansion as well.

Auto responders

These are useful so that any inquiry gets an immediate email telling the sender that their message has been received.

Company website

This can range from very simple with a brief bio of the company and contact information, to an interactive site with the capability for your customers to initiate a live chat with your customer service department.

Important Note: This may seem self-evident, but I have seen so many business websites where I have had to search for their contact information. At the very least, make sure you have your phone number and/or email address on EVERY PAGE of your website. Failing that, a "Contact Us" link, on every page, to a contact form that your customer can fill out.

Newsletters

Monthly newsletters and/or product/appointment announcements to opted-in customers to keep them up to date on what's happening with your company. There are many services out there that can make this easy and help keep track of your opted-in clients. Look into services like Aweber, iContact or Constant Contact, to name a few. These services can help make sure you aren't spamming your customers because they handle your email lists for you and will remove anyone who chooses to opt out.

My best suggestion is to take the time and effort to be certain that whatever technologies you choose can be incorporated into your company with the least amount of effort and chaos and with the most amount of return.

Empowering Your Employees

Establish clear company policies and guidelines

Too often, when I've spoken to different people at the same company, I get conflicting stories. One person will say that they can do a specific thing, but then another person will say that, no, that's not the way it is. This indicates that the company either doesn't have clear and consistent policies or that the policies have not been clearly explained to each and every employee.

What's the best way to avoid this? The company's policies should be in a WRITTEN document. Ideally, there should be an employee manual that is always up-to-date. New employees should receive one when they start and should be given company time to read it thoroughly. Existing employees should be given updates as they occur and should have a manual, either printed or electronic, that they can update easily.

Keep It Simple

Company policies should be simple, concise and easy to understand. There shouldn't be a lot of exceptions. That just muddies the waters. If you start adding a lot of "ifs", "ands" or "buts" then you'll just confuse your employees and they won't be able to convey company policies accurately to your customer base.

Ideally, a single, written page of company policies should be your goal. That will make it easy to remember and quick to refer to when necessary.

How Much Monetary Leeway Do Your Employees Have?

Sometimes an unhappy customer can be quickly turned into a happy customer with a small reduction in price or a small credit. Do your employees have the authority to do this? In most cases, they should. However, you'll need to give them very clear limits on how much leeway they have.

In some cases you may feel comfortable with your employees knowing the cost of your products. However, letting them know a percentage of the purchase price that they can play with often makes more sense.

As business owners, we know that the cost of an item isn't the whole story. Along with making a profit for each item sold, we need to pay our employees, pay the lighting and heating bills, make the mortgage payment on the building, pay phone bills and more.

Sometimes an employee doesn't think about these things and when they see the mark-up applied to the products they are selling they think the owner is making a HUGE profit, or even gouging. They just don't have all the information they need to see that that isn't the case at all.

If you are comfortable with employees knowing your cost - great. Even still, though, giving them a percentage to work with is often much easier and they won't be tempted to give away all of the profit!

In my experience, I've found that if they know they can give a customer a 5% to 10% discount, depending on the item, they are very comfortable with that. It also gives them the ability to make a decision without having to tell the customer that they have to check with their manager first. Putting a customer "on hold" while an employee has to check with a manager gives the customer lots of time to simply change their minds. Immediate decisions are much better.

Return Policies

Any return policies also need to be clearly communicated to every employee. Be sure to set policies on such things as:

❖ If any item accepted for return must be in the original box, unused and resalable

❖ If returns are not accepted on special order items

❖ If your company imposes a restocking charge

❖ If there is a time limit on returns

❖ If the original receipt is required for returns

❖ If you only allow exchanges or credits, but not cash refunds

These, of course, are just suggestions - just something to get you thinking about return policies. What I'm really trying to say is that, whatever your return policy is, all of your employees need to be totally clear on what that is.

REWARDING YOUR EMPLOYEES

IT'S NOT ALWAYS ABOUT MONEY.

Most often, when companies think about rewarding their employees, the first thing that comes to mind is a raise or, perhaps, a bonus. Don't get me wrong, these are great ideas. However, monetary compensation seems to have a limited shelf life.

Let me explain. With a raise, your employee will quickly get used to living up to the new income. We all do that. With a bonus, it will likely get spent rather than saved and then the reward is gone. Most of us would also do the same. This isn't ungrateful behavior, it's just normal.

PAY YOUR EMPLOYEES WELL

If you have a good employee, pay them well. The best advice I have ever heard on this was from a boss I had very early in my career. He told me that if you pay a good employee more than they can get elsewhere, they will stay.

Your employee's standard pay level should reflect their value to your company. Don't use pay raises as short term rewards.

SO, HOW SHOULD YOU REWARD EMPLOYEES?

If you want to recognize some exceptional behavior or an amazing review from a customer, think a little outside the box. Try giving them something that they wouldn't normally give themselves or, perhaps, couldn't afford to fit into their budget.

❖ *A weekend for your employee and their significant other at a local Inn or Bed & Breakfast*

❖ *A night out with dinner and live theatre*

❖ *A day at a spa - with the royal treatment*

"PERSONAL ANECDOTE"

One company that I worked with paid my airfare so that I could spend Christmas with my family one year. That was almost 30 years ago and I still remember it and talk about it. That kind of reward creates lasting memories and with it lasting gratitude and appreciation.

PRAISE IN PUBLIC, CRITICIZE IN PRIVATE

Having been on both sides of the fence - as an employee and an employer - I am in the unique position to see this from both sides.

PRAISE IN PUBLIC

Publicly praising your employees creates a positive atmosphere. If employees know that they will be recognized for "going the extra mile" then they are more likely to do it and other employees are more likely to follow suit.

Praising an employee in front of a customer creates a positive impression on both the customer and the employee.

Just like customers, employees need to feel valued, appreciated and listened to.

CRITICIZE IN PRIVATE

Any criticism you feel you need to give your employee - constructive or not - is best done behind closed doors.

Public criticism can just as easily be called public humiliation. And that usually doesn't end well.

If you berate an employee in front of other employees, customers, or both, the atmosphere quickly turns uncomfortable, negative and, sometimes, downright hostile.

We've all seen the type of boss that figures berating an employee in public, often loudly, will whip the troops into shape and impress the customers. It doesn't. DON'T DO IT!

What it actually accomplishes is making the boss, and by extension, the company, look unreasonable, uncaring and just generally grumpy. But the worst of these is making the company look bad - to both the customers and the employees.

Remember - without customers there is no company and without employees, you can't run your company.

😃 Happy customers will buy your products.

😃 Happy employees will make it easy for the customers to buy your products.

😃 Happy employees are more productive, more positive and exude confidence.

😃 Happy employees will go above and beyond if necessary, and do so willingly.

😃 Happy employees promote the positives of your company because they are positive about your company.

Constructive Criticism

Another thing to remember when you feel the need to criticize an employee, constructive criticism goes a lot further and leads to less resentment.

When instructing employees on how to do something better, or more inline with company policy, it's a good idea to let them know that you also notice the things they are doing right and not just the areas that need improvement. An honest pat on the back before suggesting ways to improve in other areas will put your employee in a much better frame of mind to accept any corrections for areas of their performance that may be lacking.

When an Employee is not a Good Fit for Your Company

There will be times that you'll have to let an employee go. I hope that this is a difficult thing for you to do. I know that any time I've had to do this I've agonized over it for days and generally got very little sleep during that time.

Sometimes an employee is just not a good fit - help that employee look for another position - whether within your company or not - do not just fire them and cut them loose.

By helping an employee find another, more suitable, position, you'll also gain the respect of your other employees. They'll realize that you and your company are both caring and loyal and won't just "hang them out to dry".

Remember - if you want loyalty, be loyal.

❧ ♥ ❧

In this bonus chapter, written specifically for managers/owners, you've learned the following:

✔ *How leading by example can be an effective management tool*

✔ *The need to explore technology to aid in customer service*

✔ *How empowering your employees is good for your company*

✔ *How to reward employees in unique ways other than just money*

✔ *The correct way to praise and criticize your employees*

At Geezer Guides we not only talk the talk, we walk the walk. We believe in what Victoria teaches 100%. Please contact us if we can help in any way.

Check out our other titles at:

http://ebooks.geezerguides.com

ABOUT THE AUTHOR

Victoria Wells has been in the customer service field for over 30 years. She has a unique perspective on the role of a customer service representative as, throughout her career, she has been an employee, an employer and a consultant.

Victoria has had the opportunity and the privilege to work with many different companies in diverse fields.

She felt that a simple, common sense, no-nonsense guide to a career in customer service was missing from all the training books and manuals available.

Her writing style is chatty and non-threatening. She uses experiences from her own career to highlight, and bring clarity to, the advice she offers.

You can contact Victoria directly at:

vicky@geezerguides.com

Please Review

I hope you have enjoyed this book and will post a favorable review. Independent authors rely on feedback from readers like you to spread the word about books you enjoy. You can leave your comments and contact the author directly by visiting the Geezer Guides web site.

Geezer Guides (the publisher of this book) frequently promotes new titles by offering free copies on special one day only sales. As one of my readers I would like you to get all my new books without charge. Just visit http://ebooks.geezerguides.com and get on their mailing list by filling out the simple form there.

OTHER BOOKS FROM GEEZER GUIDES

http://ebooks.geezerguides.com/book/second-time-around/

http://ebooks.geezerguides.com/book/how-to-make-perfect-pastry-dough-every-time/

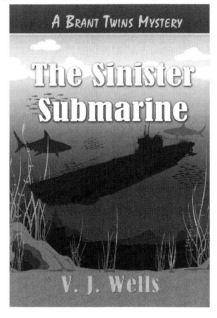

http://ebooks.geezerguides.com/book/the-sinister-submarine/

http://ebooks.geezerguides.com/book/how-to-create-format-publish-promote-profit-from-the-ebook-opportunity/

http://ebooks.geezerguides.com/book/high-fat-high-calorie-delicious-five-volume-set/

http://ebooks.geezerguides.com/book/how-to-make-authentic-english-recipes-the-complete-collection/

Common Sense Customer Service

65649318R00040

Made in the USA
San Bernardino, CA
04 January 2018